You May Not Take the Sad and Angry Consolations

Also by SHANE NEILSON

Poetry

New Brunswick

Dysphoria

On Shaving Off His Face

Complete Physical

Meniscus

Non-Fiction

Constructive Negativity: Prize Culture, Evaluation, and Dis/ability

Margin of Interest: On English Language Poetry of the Maritimes

Gunmetal Blue

Call Me Doctor

Fiction

Will

SHANE NEILSON

You May Not Take the Sad and Angry Consolations

icehouse poetry
an imprint of Goose Lane Editions

Copyright © 2022 by Shane Neilson.

All rights reserved. No part of this work may be reproduced or used in any form or by any means, electronic or mechanical, including photocopying, recording, or any retrieval system, without the prior written permission of the publisher or a licence from the Canadian Copyright Licensing Agency (Access Copyright). To contact Access Copyright, visit accesscopyright.ca or call 1-800-893-5777.

Edited by Jim Johnstone.
Cover and page design by Julie Scriver.
Cover image by Devn, @heydevn on Instagram.
Excerpt from *O Fallen Angel* by Kate Zambreno reprinted by permission of HaperCollins Publishers LLC.
Excerpt from *The Triumph of Love* by Geoffrey Hill. Copyright © 1998 by Geoffrey Hill. Reprinted by permission of Mariner Books, an imprint of HarperCollins Publishers LLC.
Printed in Canada by Rapido.
10 9 8 7 6 5 4 3 2 1

Library and Archives Canada Cataloguing in Publication

Title: You may not take the sad and angry consolations / Shane Neilson.
Names: Neilson, Shane, 1975- author.
Description: Poems.
Identifiers: Canadiana 20210292687 | ISBN 9781773102481 (softcover)
Classification: LCC PS8577.E33735 Y58 2022 | DDC C811/.6—dc23

Goose Lane Editions acknowledges the generous support of the Government of Canada, the Canada Council for the Arts, and the Government of New Brunswick.

Goose Lane Editions
500 Beaverbrook Court, Suite 330
Fredericton, New Brunswick
CANADA E3B 5X4
gooselane.com

Behold, O Lord; for I am in distress: my bowels are troubled; mine heart is turned within me; for I have grievously rebelled: abroad the sword bereaveth, at home there is as death.

    — Lamentations 1:20

Contents

Epistemology 9

ONE You May Not Take the Sad and Angry Consolations

Shame-Trick 13
Never-Trick 14
No-Trick 15
Obligation-Trick 16
Fear-Trick 18
Satisfaction-Trick (Permission Granted) 21

NEW YORK MINUTE
Fatherhood-Trick 23
You may not take the sad and angry consolations. 25
In the famous American art gallery 26
Freedom-Trick 27
Protection-Trick 29
Beauty-Trick 32
Disbelief-Trick 34
Death-Trick 36

TWO Take Everything, but Leave the Flowers

Deep Religious Faith 39
Hell around the Flowers 41
Driving across Pennsylvania, I Had a Great Notion 44
To All My Followers, I Propose the Photosynthesis-Dopamine Hypothesis 47

THREE The Weeping Tense

Faithless in Hospitals 51
The Weeping Tense 52
Lion Parachute 53

Small snippets to unremember undoing 55

My heart breaks in the NYPL, but it was already broken, truly —
    I just stumbled on the pieces 56

At the Met to Die Again 58

Whitman on Twitter 60

Que sera 61

One's Self I Sing, Too 62

e pluribus unum per cent 63

I was like you, once 65

The angel, running out the door again 66

Next to Edgar Allan Poe House and Museum, closed to the public
    for renovations 68

Scripture in De Witt Clinton Park 69

Crossing Myself in Rutherford, NJ 70

The Hostage Tells a Love Story (Mental Health Check) 73

Epistemology

Why does it hurt when emotion spills out of a body? How does emotion spell "body"? What does it mean to be good? Why is the surplus of beauty everywhere? What is the password? Is there always another way? What is the real word for "real"? Is there room for one more? Is it meant to be? What is the subject to time? Why are the painful questions four words long or less? Why steel, steel, steel? Where is the path? What is a story? How much more loss? Is this the end? Who are the dead? Is there a reason? Is it safe? What remains?

What about me? Am I good? Where can I hide? Am I allowed? Am I in one piece? Am I alive? What's in it for me? Where can I trade less for more? Am I being objective here? Do I have to accept this? What does my father's face mean? Can I escape? Can I take it with me when I go? Can I wake up now? Can I see change when it is coming or only when nothing is the same? What is my role in this disaster? Am I right or wrong? Did I choose that? Am I responsible? What do I know? All my life: what do I know?

When I say need, what do you hear? Can you hear me? Do you have a secret? Are you talking to me? I know you are, but what am I? Will you miss me? If I told you, would you believe me? Can I ask you a question? Will you take care of me? If I needed you, would you come? Can I help you? Why do you hate me so much? How can I do better? What can I get for you? Can you show me? Why do you talk about me that way? Will you hurt me and go on hurting me? Can I count on you? Will you let me go? Do you believe in me? When will you give me what I want?

Where do you hide? Will you wait? Where will you go? Why did you fuse the words "pain" and "love"? Were you born in a field, or sui generis? How do you see yourself? Do you even have a plan? How do you get out of bed in the morning? Did you think for just one second? Are you high? What is your problem? Are you sure? Do you care? Why am I asking? Are you serious? How bad do you want it? Are you all in? Are you protecting yourself? Are you insane? Are you both the rhyme and reason? Are you both terrible act and the turning season?

Who is included in "we"? Do we belong here? Are we there yet? Can we stop now? Do we look at the sky hoping for deliverance? Can we heal in story? Where did everyone go? Why must we fail? Why are we afraid? Do we prefer strength? Can we be serious for a second? How did we get here? Can we work this out together? Were we meant to be together? Can we split the difference? Should we? Do we have common ground or is it in another year, another season? Yes. Another season. Are we in agreement? Is there anything else we can argue about?

ONE
You May Not Take the Sad and Angry Consolations

Shame-Trick

Shame-trick was improvised by Want, who demanded a system.

His minions: *Our System Makes You Feel Bad Because We Are Bad.*

The shame-trick is purer than original sin; it is Want recast as Blame from within.

Good things now evince cringe.

Long ago, the shame-trick renovated forgiveness into an apocalypse of injury and correction.

To ask, *What happened at the start of us?* is part of the predictive system.

Answers thrown backward begin as: *Always*. And *Forever*.

The shame-trick trains us to prearrange flesh then throws itself forward as fire.

Look, the system is visible in transfers — love chased from body to body because we are *not good, not good, not good*, the beautiful arcs spread golden and bodily, away —

*

You may not take.

You may not take the condemned thing and condemn it again.

You may not take the sad and angry consolations.

You may not take the orientation to the sun, the spiritual photosynthesis that is not moral.

You may not take the old concept of soul and rip it from my wish.

You may not take the shame-trick, the revision of this world that shall be dismantled (but not shamed) for being a beautiful solution to Want.

*

We need the shame-trick's ruins to learn other tricks, but we need ruins first.

Here are all the other tricks.

Never-Trick

Always. Forever.

It has always been.

It feels like forever.

Cracks spread across the face of my watch; sun smacks the dial.

Time is biased against change — the promise of the way it was, is, and will be.

The system reduces choice to perfect postures — absorbing blows, sweeping the street clean.

O children who must take care, know that freedom and control are both invisible, equally.

If I say, *I am controlled by spirit*, then understand the contradiction.

*

Daughters, slip under the stream to save your brief, tricked life: *I want to be free.*

Son, dip your head as self-baptism and scream: *Free!*

In the system, water is always thrown behind fire by bodies bending down to be burned, bodies bent in perverse assent.

Next time you Always your life and Forever a past, resolve to fall in love with the choice that you can love.

Tie ribbons to your noose.

Never is lost in the stream and your scent is lost to the system.

Shame loses permanent chronology.

No-Trick

No is authority, power.

(No is said to the self, like all other words.)

No to the child, no to the parent, no to the God, no to the air.

No is time held still, three tenses incinerating the world.

And yet, "Burn Nobly," said Giordano Bruno.

No said often enough creates a deafness to sad and angry consolations.

No is thinking that I can hold Zee, Kaz, and Aria no matter what comes.

But no is what comes, and *No!* is the word I'll scream underwater instead of *Free!*

No is not resistance, either.

*

You may not take the consolations because I question yes — the threshold overwhelmed.

Obligation-Trick

Oh, you must love.

You Must.

Programmed into your first cry is that first obligation — You Must.

Systematic.

Trying to resist was your first and best No.

This No transformed into shame.

You didn't want to love *them*, but you had to.

Not to love is *bad, so bad, bad*, every good thing crushed under a crowd of feet fleeing in relays —

Every cry directed outward, every need — satisfied and unsatisfied — is participation.

Remember, shame is not your fault.

The best of us is dust rearranged into foreordained shapes, love's perfect body.

*

The laughter here is a husk. Enough of that sound! Our laughs must not exaggerate, must state that we hurt — and hurt enough.

We dream in forms of wonder (meant for others). The sound of wonder grinds against astonishment.

A head comes off-its-head. What I have held in my hand was first withheld.

Laugh at answers, because we are now beyond framing questions.

*

Need is systematic, need in anticipation of correction, need arrayed into love and love's obligation —

The best of us transformed into chalk, silt after fire —

                        so sing with chalk in your throat / burn nobly / varnish desire with the silt,

              and the best of us will no longer be dust, and our obligation will only be to sing,

                                                                         to sting —

Fear-Trick

I can't remember now, what house is it again?

It was written: *we are bad, so bad, bad . . .*

And the echo underwritten is: *love, must love, love . . .*

Fear keeps the tense single, three-in-one: afraid of skin, knowledge sharpened to sculpt our postures, terrified of the blow that comes, is coming, has come, and predicts the future . . .

Loss is an exact coordinate, the body with its right hand outstretched, pleading *No*, the left blinding . . .

Fear commissions the devil to police the garden.

Fear is colourless *Havoc* that removed Want from the throne.

Ask yourself: what do I want?

The answer is: *I want the not*. I want not to be afraid.

The devil smells fear.

A lie broadcast in the burning garden: Safety is the First Want.

Head one fathom deep in the river and you are safe — uncoupled from fear, quiet as Heraclitus. O my deep deep love Heraclitus,

you cannot burn, cannot burn, you cannot burn

         — you never burned, never burned, you never burned —

freedom the difference between   incandescence/incombustible   consumed/consuming
         noble

What have I become?

When you feel fear, sense system instead, cast it out with a word, with your head engulfed.

Free —

*

You may not take what did not happen, what is not happening, what will not happen —

Free —

You may not take the ruins, the unconstructed self, the system's implements that make for terrible shelters, worship conducted in torture chambers —

You may not take the lancinating urge to wonder if anything else should be built in another name —

*

My daughter, my son, and my daughter, I relinquish you —

Remember the space to be burned is small.

Someone will love you there, draw you there with love, someone who wants to be good, who started in goodness long ago, but love will relinquish you from that chamber.

The space to be burned is small, but hunger wide —

Water eats strange thoughts, overwhelms sense —

Free —

Remember you are free.

I wish, I give you freedom;

I can only say it is there, in the ruins: that you are good,

Good, so good, good

*

You may not take shame, fear, refusal.

The system is what you want, removed from what you can get.

In the ruinous self, freedom can be found.

It was always there, is there, will be —

Want polices the ruinous self —

                                            Plunge your head —

Satisfaction-Trick (Permission Granted)

Haven't we all used protractors to make black holes, only to return to hear the music, yet hating the need for music?

We blame the things that save us.

Some call this *method*, but I name it, "not knowing how the trick is done, and rejoicing it is yet performed."

I've walked in the wood too often to wonder why the way home is the way home. Some animals have an instinct to die and I have the same.

My mother hid from the world to die. Before I die, I will hide behind a chair like I did when I was a child. You will find me there, not wanting to bother anyone.

Some say the proper word is *miracle*, others say *mystery* — I say the proper term is *strangeness*.

In the *OED*, the suffix *-ness* comes from Old English — and means *to make even*.

Oh, please do as I say, not as I do — and read otherwise —

I wake next to your mother each morning. Arms around her, I feel like I've cheated death again, with no idea how it was done. The reward is not to know.

Reprieve: to cancel or postpone punishment. The closest I've come to the secret are three fragments:

> *never any shields —*
>
> we all have so little time together —
>
> there are those, too, who suffer grave emotional and mental disorders, but many of them recover if they have the capacity to be honest —

Be welcome in these three.

There are no medicines and no definitions adequate for our condition.

To hear the wrong song with the wrong mind — such *risk*.

The word *succumb* denies the work of sad and angry consolations.

If numb from pain, ask yourself: why meet the maker with gold? Clutch the tin can, root,
and dysphoric syllabus.

Blame these things, but they save strangeness that's too terrible to quell with anesthetics —

To die with all three of you in love is the consolation I want most, but the advance nightmare is:
one of you walks into the vale and does not return, for want of method.

I couldn't save myself from myself either, but I learned my three charms — and O loves
to have lifted you in my arms and heard you sing through the old houses, it was only goodness

— I blame myself —

for we are connected to death, others cannot understand

I understand

Forsake shame.
Be honest.
The tragedy is to hasten before the satisfaction.
The trick is, always, to wait until the next morning.

To be *with*

You have my blessing then
only then, and then

NEW YORK MINUTE

Fatherhood-Trick

I'm forty-two, just before my death. I feel it in the floor and the towers of New York, its railway tracks and neoliberal boutiques

Heraclitus is skipping rocks on the Hudson, and he disapproves of my taking the Lincoln Tunnel

Against the skyline, the universe ponders the morals of mortals

> *Point to the place it hurts*, I said after your thousand individual, little falls

> (I once jumped from the top of an apartment building)

> I hurt all over

Years ago, a consultant sent a patient back to my office with a note: *Mrs. X says they have "total body pain." I can't help them with total body pain!*

Person as wound? Not the right metaphor. Poem as wound? Too familiar.

Zee wants to go shopping on the Lower East Side

Kaz was photographed with Minions and Mickey Mouse in Times Square

Aria plays with a Happy Meal toy — it's Baseball Snoopy that shoots out a token —

And every second there is a whisper in my ear, the words are unimportant

Some call this suffering, but the strangeness is: I'm already dead

The priest can't help with total body pain

Why take a photograph of this for you to see? Poem as wounding.

> (I still dream of the water tower, it is a monument to desire)

In the hospital too long ago, I took a picture of my face as proof of death-in-life. The image displays the selfsame sickness we all must wear, the familiar token —

Some songs throw out my mind and I give up

I need a poem that's total-body-pain, I need the selfsame thing

To show you that I know, I do know — and even in the middle of the mightiest reasons to go on — *you* — the whisper occurs through the song, *water tower, water tower*

I sting you —

And some songs are no help at all, they are cessation

Medicine has its limits

I am delimited

And though I felt blessed with you, I still want to die for the pain

There is not enough for the pain. Ask the bodies

> I am not enough for you, but I had to stand in place of, I had to be put for —
> some other metaphor,
> some other fatherhood

All the brick in this city, fire escapes and billboards, horns and gods

It was never fair, my demands cloaked as wishes for you to be yourselves, to be *free*

I couldn't save me, why should you stand in place of, be put for —

And yet you did the trick — how monstrous to say

Be good, it's all I can say, *be good* — I put nothing in place of that, I lose track of the whisper, of myself

You may not take the sad and angry consolations.

You may not take the **sad** and **angry** consolations.

You may not **take** the sad and angry consolations.

You may not take the sad and angry **consolations**.

You may not take the sad and angry consolations.

You **may not** take the sad and angry consolations.

In the famous American art gallery

In the famous American art gallery, *they* are looking at *The Starry Night*.
In the famous American art gallery, I am looking at *them*.

What do we see in painting and audience? The same blue whorls of light, the same blue light that spins the galaxy, the same registrations.

In the famous American art gallery, I understand the power of myth. *They* speak of ears and the postal service.

other / other / other / other / other / other / other / other / other / other / other / other / other

In the famous American art gallery, the starry night is consumed.
In the famous American art gallery, the cellphones offer knives to Van Gogh, offer to finish the job.

Somewhere in the famous American art gallery, my wife is feeding our daughter.
Next to me in the famous American art gallery, Zee is watching me watch *them*.

In the famous American art gallery, I detect neither empire nor falling empire,
                                                love nor love's end,
                                                        my fellow ill or good American teeth.

In the famous American art gallery, I see yet another archive of the sad and angry consolations.

Freedom-Trick

Shall I rejoice in *never*, in *no*? No word is intrinsically *bad, so bad, bad* — I shall.

Do I contradict myself?

Very well then, I contradict myself.

Freedom has a sting.

Don't lift your head from the water too soon.

My mother, at the end of her life, could not breathe — pure oxygen, her head under water.

Feel the body's ultimate strain before succumbing to air.

Otherwise, freedom stops being the crack in the bell, and it becomes perfected with fists and prison bars.

Leveraged hearts as sanctified good, so good, as love?

It is not love; it is trickery.

If your chest seizes as you read this, if it tightens and your throat closes, then your body understands.

I couldn't breathe either at the end of her life.

Freedom pressed on my neck.

Never let freedom lose its sting.

*

Do not mistake the sting for freedom itself.

Turn away from what you love for a moment, and if you want to turn back, then it might be true.

What to say at the end of my life?

I fought for you to be free, I stung you —

Yes, pain can be freedom and trickery both —

Remember the feeling in your chest, your neck, the sting of looking away and looking back —

and the river that's there for you —

Protection-Trick

Protect children.

Cite protection as the means to wake and be in the world. Run from fire to fire and extinguish them with irrigating care.

My homicidal fantasy: I would destroy schoolyard bullies, taunters, the tricky ones, my fist shattering their cricoids, their skulls open on the brick, with the court duly told: *I would do the same thing again to fulfill my function as father.*

But the secret is: I cannot protect myself, so this fear is a transposed positive, rendered into a good.

Is it good, to gather and keep?

Your faces tell me a thousand times, yes; to keep you, to protect you, to suffer the little children, but you need protection from more than others & violence. These are the lesser.

Moreso from the beauty-trick: that poisons are beautiful, and are beautiful because the recipe calls for the poisonous.

I act in the name of beauty but declare *a thousand times yes* to say no to a thousand times ago.

*

The sun rushes into the room, on my head and hand — my son beside me, watching television — we are both lost — he is laughing —

*

A challenge from Robert Bly: "If a rhetorical poet tries to describe something as simple as a moose running, he can't do it; he is thrashing around on the ground."

A thousand *yes*es on their triggers as the moose topples, blurting out the mirrored terror: rhetorics of *assent* from its dying, ecstatic lips, their *yes*es on spasmed turbulences of dirt and coalesced mixes of spit,

me in the school field, hurling children as protection spell, you on my back, screaming —

Smite them —

But you would not. You would be human shields, screaming

Whatever you do, you do this unto me —

All three of you, waving me away.

Here is the charm against beauty: once upon a time the story ended once upon a time. Now everyone is gone — I sent them away. I write odes in the names of others and fantasy, but in the field that is once upon a time, in the discipline of once upon a time, in that science, you (once) were happy, the beauty-smears were on your shirt and you convulsed on the ground, all the rhetorics on the trigger, and one heaving breath away was the lie of a Möbius strip that refused to tell its fortune

and you were happy you were alone; the word *beautiful* forsook the world; you were happy because the rhetorics missed

> and you were finally safe

*

The only protection spell I know is that you are unprotected

> *never any shields, never any shields, never any shields*

Erect the columbaries of lies and love, and mortar the schoolyard brick with *never any shields*;

fertilize the school field with *never any shields*;

your fist reaches apotheosis when it reaches for rhetoric as shield.

Childhood cannot yield to this advice, as I yield to you flagging the field with waving arms, *We are free, free of you, we do not need you, we do not need you to feel free —*

*

Wrists bent back, knees bent, hair in his eyes, my son laughs —

*

You may not take that from me, this is my defiance, my own protection spell, my sad and angry sharing with the felled —

Once upon a time, once upon a time, once upon a time —

The best line John McCrae wrote: "loved and were loved, and now we lie"

Once upon a time you,

Once upon a time I,

Once upon a time I just wanted time to stop and for you to be preserved,

and time saved you, protected you from

*

O lord I am working towards my death

And You Know

There Are

Never Any

Beauty-Trick

Definitions first:

> (1) dirt-life squirming towards a yellow-bricked river through austere fields of extermination; that which illuminates also burns; that which quenches also drowns;

> (2) change makes contingent covenants; an eternity of injury and calculation
>
> divided by
>
> eternities of return; all human bodies and their grotesque designs; movement in darkness; not opposites, but incorporated wholes.

*

Children, I warn of proportion.

In the greatest good is the greatest injury, in the horrible act is the saving turn.

Do not succumb to false orthodoxies. Do not succumb to Beauty.

Rather, run and gather all the beautiful things that exist as a condition of that existence.

Taste them.

Other philosophies contain this advice, but note they, too, do not contain the word *versus*.

Beauty does not inform a good-versus-evil struggle, but rather is a property of matter and time.

You will be seduced by classical Beauty — it is the simplest kind.

Seek partners that are beautiful and good, because Beauty willed this, but!

Beauty is not good; it is the screen. Neither animal nor object, but condition —

*

Do not confuse Beauty with safety, for Beauty is

> (3) that we die; that we are bitten at the breast; that we are branded by those that profess to

love and protect but perform symmetries of injury, whole lineages with the preserved flaw; and O love, who would claim you are not antiquity's rose and rose's thorn; who would claim you are not modernity's vulnerable image transmitted to lethal screens; who would make a claim on you, or for you, except to want your subjects to beware the crown's sharp imprint;

    that the confused, beautiful;
    the purposeful, beautiful;
    the sad and angry consolations, beautiful.

May you find consolation in knowing that Beauty has no province of safety, no spell of protection utterable as its condition.

Protection is foolish, a fool's wish — a father's voice filling stinging lists, each entry genuine and in Beauty's own inventory.

Run —

Disbelief-Trick

Children, there will be an account from *Further Hades*. You will have a choice: to die, which is to deny the teller; or to live, which is to believe them.

Consider this account to be borne by the bearer of good tidings of some greater, unfathomable pain, one that gives you the good news of how you might be, *If*.

The pain comes roaring in. The bearer touches your ignorant head with their index finger, and you are blown back a hundred feet.

You see and feel that infinity in a moment and now are that *If*.

I'm gone now; your transformation wrote me out of my cherished delusion of Protector. I died in this new version, and you encountered another account, events that repeal young destinies: You're a raped child. Or you've been locked in an attic for most of your life. Or there is a hurter who insists on marking your body with deliberation. Every second that you breathe, you see your abuser's face and you know that you will die.

O Children, there is no moral dimension to *Further Hades*. It is a function of time and not of space, for the spaces are the improbable things, even when viewed. For example, go back to the spaces of your pain, and disbelieve your own minor tale, as mine is a minor tale, too, in perspective.

But close your eyes and see your nightmare again, all in a single moment — and you cannot breathe — and with the small breath you have left, you whisper *so good, good, so good* as a rosary —

I ask for one thing only, as single obligation — I would like you to care for one another; I would like you to fight for one another as I would fight, smiting interlopers in my sad, lonely moral dimension; but I ask only one other thing:

As much as you can, believe the person who bears the account of *Further Hades*. You will do your life's work in these moments. So much goodness, *so good, so good* —

You will be honoured with these moments.

It will be me coming to you. It will not be me coming to you. It will be the spirit of everyone and everything. It will be the whole world, screaming an immense need.

If you succumb to the disbelief-trick, remember not that I have made a single request, but instead that you were once small and that I disbelieved your most true tale. A hateful cast settled upon our lives, and it was your task to remove the husk; little lives cocooning and breaking out of the cocoons year after year, only to emerge some year in *Further Hades* —

To soothe; or to extinguish, *If*.

Death-Trick

Do we die
to serve?

*

I chase the ghost nowhere, for everything.

Do I chase myself?

I wish childhood was the answer for every hurt-box on the page, but the correct answer is We All Have So Little Time Together.

Let's say "We All Have So Little Time Together" out loud, on our knees, in unison.

Then go to work where we touch a smartphone to find an app that divides people by time.

Call it PeopleTime.

*

Close your eyes.

I'm half-past-dead and the ghosts won't be chased.

They haunt by disappearing forever.

Which is why I look. Which is the reason for pain — wanting what I can't have.

I'm ready for my close-up in dreamland:
"We All Have So Little Time Together."

I'm off my prayerful knees and running through the streets. All of these people! All of this so-called love! And we're dead in forgetting, forgetting the dead.

Here's an app: the Poem. Self-improvement is memorization, recitation.

I bless you, bless you, as so good, as free —

TWO
Take Everything, but Leave the Flowers

Deep Religious Faith
after William Carlos Williams

What can I tell you of the flowers?
I cannot know the flowers — I can tell you
I cannot know

Once upon a time, I knew the meaning
of *immanence*. But now that word
is blankets and gauze.

Great poets, were you moved by the feeling
that roils through time, an invention
of the mortal for the gods?

Mortar for the mortal: *I don't know.*
How to summon one simple
flower? An image

of building blocks, image
of a stumbling man carrying a bouquet.
Or bouquets — what time do I have?

The listeners are too quiet to be the intended audience.
This great secret:

not love for one another,
nor even respect,
but the flowers occur and recur, are precursor and recourse,

are war, curse, core, scourge — and succour.
This is transformation.
This is the difference between truth and delusion.

This is the end of my life;
I grew in darkness,
and a moral chemical let me respond to the light.

Did I grow towards it?

Let the icons fall on rosehips —
let the juries deliberate on orchids —
let the poets devote themselves to horticulture and metrics

and invent fascinating systems made of the old materials.
Go ahead, young one.
Describe.

Was I kind, as flowers can be a kindness?
Is the metaphor more camphor
than ichor, more metastasis

than electrophoresis, more thing than process,
more a religion of what is not (hate)
than what is (love)?

Or a balance of blankets and gauze? More apocalypse
than immanence? I do not know
one from the other.

Aroseisaroseisarose.
What is the oldest thing to say, the kindest,
and does it come as question or lullaby?

When I say *Transform*, the outcome cannot be controlled.
Otherwise, I would know too much —
nothing of flowers

or of worship, for the flowers
grow beyond the altar
and the stumbling man.

Please, I'm begging you — listen:
the image is a metaphor
and the metaphor is a prayer

that transforms into
the praying —

Hell around the Flowers

Was I cheered when
I learned that hell grew
around the flowers?

The flowers and their
beauty revealed nothing.
Hell told me everything:

garden metaphors are
distractions meant to lull
you down the path; keep

your face to the fire,
think instead of city.
Think grave, think the crest
of a wave that shoves

your head five fathoms deep
and enjoy your dive.
Why oh why oh why?

   I

         — horrible, sick and slick with self I, hell-bound wheeling I, singed and fixated on the beautiful as if it were palliative and not revelation —

   I

         — the dunce, I the disabled, I the author of my own misfortune and recorder of the visitations, I the awful self spreading out to infect the closest stranger with affect, the hell that grows around the flower —

   I

came up clutching flowers
and wanted them to be
the seed that resisted hell,

a seaweed that transforms
into the most resolute of loves,
some symbol that forces

the saddest of us to irrigate
hell with our tears. In each
of my poems, I ask: why tell lies?

We have so little time
together. I'm dying,
quickly — as if a moment

crashes down on my head,
and only the bottom
leaves room to survive.

And thrive? The voice low
down that makes the waves
agitate and rise —

millions of hands holding asphodels,
flowers holding hands. Every ritual
predicated on the flower.

       I

still stumble with bouquet in hand,
an old man with the news in his ears,
refusing the hot siege around the flowers.

Systems systematize resistance;
flowers are taxonomized;
beauty is in excess —

so says the death drive.

And yet I *feel* this —
an ounce of my history
would throw you down

five fathoms —

the flowers, having grown,
know better than to love,
to claim a solvent in the soul,

to pretend that we are the same,
fused —
and for the hellions, I leave

you to your claim: "I love you
or I do not live at all."
You do not live.

I cannot be the flower
or know it, because it is beautiful,
it is already dead,

and I know the dying,
the rituals based on flowers,
the praying —

Driving across Pennsylvania, I Had a Great Notion

Driving across Pennsylvania, "If It Makes You Happy"
comes on the radio. I feel as poor as the scene: ragged wildflowers,

flags & fading Second Amendment signs cresting scrub hills:
We shall not be infringed! But lo, it is from the lunatic fringe

that I come. With the red, white, and blue legacy tattoo
multiplying on rundown Americana, and three schoolchildren

in the back seat wondering why Daddy's blasting music
on the drive home, reserving their god-given right to free speech

and protest, I begin to cry. *If it makes you happy, then why the hell
are you so sad?* One reason: in the American grain are the flowers.

A day earlier, at the Top of the Rock, a couple wed elaborately,
the tuxedoed groom throwing the train in the air for photographs. *Now!*

the bride ordered, and he released diaphany. She was alabaster,
white grit, the flaw in the system that makes perfection work, this flaw:

Power must be drunk down by Love's lips to birth the State.
To the left side of the couple were bouquets of hydrangeas and lilies.

I want to lie, say the sky was rundown, too, all the drama of New York
tawdry, ramshackle, like country music pulsing heartfelt from a battered

back deck in New Brunswick, but I spitefully report instead
that it was as beautiful. The crowd's eyes were on the train

& veil in the wind against the Empire State and none on the red
and white basis that is my understanding of Crow's song — flowers,

flags, the mutually assured self-destruction that is, uniquely, American
love. *So what if everything's wrong?* An AM-radio announcer informs us:

*In Lexington Park, a boy and a girl have been shot at Great Mills High
School by another student who had a prior relationship with the girl.*

Love's lives, infringed forever. In the article I checked later to confirm
the shooting, it said: *The notion of "it can't happen here" is no longer a notion.*

This, too, from one of love's penitentials: *Sometimes I lives
in the country, sometimes I lives in the town. Sometimes I haves*

a great notion to jump in the river an' drown. With my face
as End-Is-Nigh sign, hydrangeas my headrest on the roof of Empire,

and under the dome of shared consumption, of blue, I finally understand.
God, I do. Flowers against the face feel good, and we want the good

to be our right. Later, I step into the Guggenheim's reading room
and learn more about a country reserving the right to make mistakes.

This choice origami flower in soft hands: Rockwell's *Four Freedoms*.
Thesis: O Empire, I agree, Freedom of Speech and Religion, yes,

wherever would we be otherwise? But Freedom from Want and Fear?
Why the horrible monopolists leaning in for their Thanksgiving feast?

I hate Rockwell's domestic white faces, even the little children!
I hate them, I want them to ride transports to consumptive Auschwitz.

Why must Maternos and Paternos look down benignly upon their brood,
two sleeping kiddos with the *Bennington Banner* mentioning the Blitz?

Christ, I cannot hate this painting enough, for it bombards
my five-year-old self each time I look. *Yes*, little me says inside,

that's just how it should be! Citizens taking good care of their littlezens!
Some great notion in *Freedom from Fear* excuses sentiment

and appeals to the shill in all of us — God, I understand! The salesman
self that hurts in Crow's song, *real low down*, all our lonely selves

tragically sad because we will it — even though we serially choose to be happy, right,
drinking until we're thirsty again? On the drive home from Times Square's

half-naked Banjo lady I resolved to inform you, Empire, that Freedom
from Want means no one will be free to speak; and if free from Fear,

I will no longer be alive; nor any of my line; nor anyone else.
For fear gives birth to children. I say to you and to those clothed in virtue:

there's no category difference between fears, only degrees.
You may not take my fears and call them freedom, nor dress up freedom

as care, *as* concern, *as* love, for this is how all war starts —
as kindness, Maternos and Paternos standing over our beds. I refuse

the bed and instead will jump, hydrangeas trailing like a veil and train
from the top of Rockefeller Center.

To All My Followers, I Propose the Photosynthesis-Dopamine Hypothesis

Fire asphodels from your mouth as if from the sleeves of third-rate magicians.

I see so much that you cannot see.

Our most basic affect forms a polarity: attraction and aversion. And our basic colour is green.

I see how we grow to the light,

  go   and   no-go.

The flowers in the field, the field of flowers — zooming in: asphodels —

I feel a marked intensification of core, the flat half shake and half shudder of never knowing whether what I see — eternity of beautiful colour and petal wing, wishes and wanting and blur of white, spatter of red against the green screen — qualifies as feeling.

I feel, O Lord, your voice in my head, but I do not see you. I see the world only, the green and threatened world of sad and angry consolations.

THREE
The Weeping Tense

Faithless in Hospitals

Despair, they said to me a long time ago, *is a mortal sin.*

Somewhere a sparrow called its mate.

Past the asphalt rectangle, grass grows into a greater, greener heaven.

All the living things genuflect at my soul's gate.

Have faith, they said to me a long time ago. And I was good. And it was good.

Then grief came for me.

Charred corpses of birds whispered in my ear, *Extinction-level event.*

Consumed, the grass could no longer point at the back of the wind, where faith blows the good things, at random, for fools.

I heard a doctor say terrible things — implacable, irreversible things.

For example: *He's beautiful*, they said. *Have faith.*

No, I said, *no. No.*

They said, *Change.*

And I said, *No! The change already happened; don't you see?*

And they said, *Nothing is different; he is your son, have faith.*

I feel the lid of the coffin creep over my back. I whisper to the wood, *You have such faith in me, such faith.*

The human ditty: beautiful, yes, such beauty in excess; with loss crashing down in wave after wave, crushing faith as if it were a child's toy boat sent out to sea.

No. Who will stand uselessly on guard for him after I am gone?

The Weeping Tense
for the listeners

There's too little light in this room.

I have something to tell you —
lean closer, I'll write more quickly,
I promise, I love you —

don't cry —

over the kitchen counter
today,
clearing scraps, I started to weep.

Out the sliding door, I could see the unkempt grass
bullied by a fleeing wind

and I thought of all the things my son is,
now.

If emotion is useless,
then each tear is:
not exorcism,
not process,
but how I can't do anything else;
inflammatory mediators throwing flags
into the brine of the future, the future, the future, the future, the future
is dripping onto the counter,
and in the fading light
we can still taste the salt
and say,
at least —

a love you can choke on, and get, heavy — wearing, grinding
at least —

so close now, your face, ear
and the future

Lion Parachute

For most of us the only way
To become a lion is to be devoured by one.
Body of a lamb, soul of a lion.

   — David McFadden

The Long Cold Blue Evenings of Spring is a title I would like to live one day, for once in this life

No armour   never any shields

What is this feeling?

And if they took away this feeling, would you be relieved? Would I?

If I said I wanted him to live,
it would not matter —

the matter
is not what's wrong,
but what *is* —

not what to do, or not what
to do or not what to
do or not what
to do or
not

holding this small living thing
and not knowing what to do or
if it will live or, not that question
but what *is* —

not stutter, but grind, a seized axle, rust's ferric hiss —

and carrying that *is* into a long cold blue evening in springtime,
coughing into the sun

I need not needing him or
I need not what to do or

I need to create that evening —

If this is sadness, then
what is sadness or what
am I doing? Then

stop the evening, not with narcotic but

with a picture of a blue lion,
blue like a child
clutching their only crayon.

Come, try to take it from me.

Small snippets to unremember undoing

This in section 67 of the New York Public Library, from Bianca Stone:

> *fumbling clear black angels, backup dancers, flawless*
> *cheerleading squad*
> *. . . . .*
> *hustling over the shipwrecked world*

Grief connects all the sad and angry consolations, snowmelt —

Recognizing that the starting position is loss, that tomorrow was never the future, never a possibility — it was a growing singularity calling me home.

So what next? My cells sing a solace of entropy, headed in the same direction of separation, checking out of the Skyline Hotel.

The truck that hits the car that kills the people in the intersection was driven by the same ghost that cooked my son's head.

The toddler that pulled the trigger to kill the grade-school sister was tricked by the same ghost

the selfsame ghost
self
same:

O Lord, O love, O why — the ghost's song.

I hear dumb pop songs and feel in the presence of a genius of feeling.

> *Flo flo little wo*
> *Flo beyo imagino*
> *The sofo clo, the who do*
> *Upo the wo of heavo's looooooo*

this, the first law of psychodynamics:
the closer we are to death, the greater we feel a pop song —

and what is home in the pop song?
My back deck —

My heart breaks in the NYPL, but it was already broken, truly—I just stumbled on the pieces

In the Whitman exhibit at the NYPL, I see primordial words: lifeblood, democracy, fellowship; but Walt, you're missing, as you've always been —

The tattered democracy continues to fly the selfsame flag, the selfsame —

Do we still believe in good and gray?

(Poets, have words electrocuted you? Words must do more than chasten, enforce. They stun you into care.)

Walt, Kaz watches the movie version of your life, as I gaze on artefacts in the heart of American power.

Shane, I tell myself, *decide to love the world under the Doctrine of Selfsame, as love's palimpsest offering secret after secret of how, why, to conquer and fall.*

So I decide to love it all — rashly, the bombs and genocide, too — because my cells agree that we, America and Shane, are selfsame. Walt, you, too…my cells encounter your counter-archival words for the republic:

> There are two attributes of the soul, and both are illimitable, and they are its north latitude and its south latitude. One of these is Love. The other is Dilation or Pride.

O Love that breaks my bones and calls me names, a sticks-and-stones
love that knows where I live, shares my Skyline Hotel bed, a cruel corporeal
ghost that loansharks the heart's pieces, Whitman knew your dimensions —
not qualities, but boundaries to keep us honest and well, postures of lovers aligned
like clock hands.

A text from my wife comes, saying, *Kaz won't leave my personal space*,
and O Love, illimitable except for the other latitude that defines your
boundary (the everlasting question from this fool: *why?*) I want an answer
for once not based in shared error and destruction, manifest destiny,
wrongness, hauntedness, hurt; my own self, an embittered colony
convinced of freedom but suspecting safety on the loose,
I want the answer from your throat even though it's choked
by opportunity's eagle. Speak then, Love, of yourself.

The good gray poet says:

> Of myself I speak. Monument is the answer, built on words to serve and chasten
> the republic, vast, moneyed, with arrogant buildings that beg for toddlers to topple
> them onto the homeless nestled against their sides on cardboard sleeping mats.
> I'm there, moving amongst the slumped and ragged forms, writing letters
> for the dying in the conflagration I initially dreamed of, then repented.
> I write love letters in the rubble as sustainable arrogance is rebuilt into tower,
> the rings of hell now vertical in new, heightening latitudes
>
> >   Yes, I've lost everything.
>
> >   Yes, I've gone mad — known as the most extreme freedom,
>
> >   and I know you don't want to hear it, but truth and beauty
> in a lower-case, ramshackle register are tugging on my gray cloak, tweaking my beard,
> I feel I'm breaking your faith now, I know you love me, but I have to tell you, Shane, I
> have to, it's love, it's Selfsame, all the hearts broken and testifying to north latitude.

Walt — or Love — I can't tell anymore — starts to write my love letter in the Met, addressing me as
  Foolish Soldier

And O Love this is the dream, that at last we are good, gray, and inconsequential,
illimitable — the selfsame

At the Met to Die Again

I wander the monuments in the Empire State and do not think of victims, per se; larceny, per se; scale, per se. I'm hurting — I just want to not be part of something, this thing; I want the good, beautiful song.

In the Met are the good things, endowments that purchase the painted flowers, the nude statues and studies, but these form the detritus of time — privilege fanning itself, saying: *I take, and take, and take, me o my o me o my* — therefore perfect for the Empire State and its crowds.

No. I gravitate to one sad and broken scene reproduced over and over — the family.

How to take in The Family as *objet*?

How does one scan Manet? Degas? Van Gogh? One does, if one is pulled to canvases with families. Forgotten is bare flesh, epic combat, landscapes —

Then I see: the fatherless, the motherless, a scene with children aged like mine — Picasso's *La Coiffure*.

Do you know why you stood at the altar, really? Isn't there mystery at the core of metaphor?

I was summoned here to not-understand, to wonder at how the children are comfortable with each other.

A domesticity of foreground, no home or other life; the boy's face at an odd slant, as if he, too, is tilted at the angle of the world, and the girls so carefully grooming beauty — the eldest arranging the middle child's hair, the middle child holding on to a blank mirror with both hands.

I could tell you *we're* the lack of background, *we're* the mirror that won't reflect; more ekphrasis can be done. But my problem's here:

the entire regiment of my body wants to protect these children, to let them be with one another unharmed; but I would want to be background, and that would ruin the picture.

I love you, my family! It is love that I feel, with every rough gesture and word! May I save you?

I may not, there is no background for that

Que sera, Doris sings to my son's temporal lobes, *Que sera*

There's only the boy in his own self, disinterested in his sisters and the background, and yet parallel to them

Is he sad? is my constant question and worry
What does he know?

Does he know more than me?
He is in the picture, next to beauty — closer than I will ever get, protected

Whitman on Twitter

I love the idea of democracy, the beautiful republic — free society.

Blah blah blah.

My friends, I sing a song of abstraction called Body. Love my body, honour it with the commerce of touch, of money changing hands —

Blah blah blah.

I wish I could disbelieve in possibility, but I cannot; I wish that love had another name, but it does not; worship the Body all day and night and remark on beauty.

Blah blah blah.

As I worship your body, as textual and sensory and intention over execution . . . even in darkness, behold — we hate one another in the most authoritarian of ways, on all sides we surround the dividing house?

Blah blah blah.

    wtf troll

Democracy as the best defence we ever had against one another (abstraction)

Democracy is not body politic, but body, love is work, the hardest work (abstraction)

All the flawed things were flawed in creation, and we must love the flaws to work to change them (abstraction)

I see myself in all the hatred; with my hands I wrought the ill and tended the soldiers' bodies both
selfsame, selfsame

When I died, there was just one word on my lips. I made sure it was the most beautiful word.
If it falls, I want that word — democracy — to whisper to the internet

Que sera

Who can take the pain away?

Que sera

If I can deliver my questions like payloads, then who will be left standing?

Que sera

Who is responsible?

Que sera

This, too, shall not pass?

Que sera —

with the void at point-blank, I peek through the black cardboard pinprick and see Doris
quell him to sleep, to sleep,
rocking him in her perfect alabaster arms,
the future's not ours to see,
and Doris looks up at me,
already pretty and rich.

Staring contest:

One's Self I Sing, Too

Of physiology from top to toe I sing,
Not physiognomy alone nor brain alone is worthy for the Muse,
    I say the Form complete is worthier far

    — Walt Whitman

As physiology informs tears, I sing.
As hate makes muscles clench, thereby moving the lymph, I sing.
As biology provides an avatar for revenge, I sing.
As the Muse is not exchangeable for outcome, I sing.
Que sera, I sing —
(and *save me* I sing *save me save me save this family save me*)
As the rabidity of the blood incites casualties, I sing —
As everyone sings, sings along, sings over, with, against,
As the moral language is bankrupt and the new vernacular is validation, I sing —
As the poor body survives the song, of the poor body I sing —
As the hierarchy of form is paramount, I sing —
As I would sell my soul for the perfect form, for the perfect is curative, preventative, outcome based,
    I sing
As my nails were picked already, I sing
As I go to bed haunted with the ghost, I sing
As the ghost and form, body and validation, cacophony, blood and muse, outcome and avatar,
    muscles and tears make an amalgam of democracy, I sing —
but am left as I started, without catharsis
only discharge

e pluribus unum per cent

If a nation expects to be ignorant and free, in a state of civilization, it expects what never was and never will be.

— Thomas Jefferson

America, I address the free who never were, who aren't, and who won't be —
in the aftermath state, in the e pluribus unum per cent of the sadness I see,
I give you back your tired, your poor, your huddled masses
yearning to breathe. Consider them for a moment.
They're bundled in rhetoric. They're sick in the grain, of the grain,
by and for the grain. They're in pain, dreaming your bootstrap dream.
I'm no better than you, or you than me — except freedom is the epithet
at the bottom of my shoe, it's a stone I'll hurl in a glass house to defenestrate
my ears and tongue. It's money as you please, the whole grease of your republic —
and again, I'm no different — I spend money, too, or deposit lucre in bank machines
and see my face reflected, blank as the basilisk. Let's play the aphorism
game. Money is truth. Truth is beauty. Beauty is truth is money is freedom.
Ignorance is bliss, a freedom from care. The good green lady is made from iron
and she bends the American will to the horizon. She's on an island that took
enough and is now closed to the information in people. Did I ever tell you
the secret of how I came to be? No less steeped in ignorance
or founding fathers themselves seeking some land to enact laws and ensure
that the newest edict was the greatest edict — with respect, I write this!
They forget the f in law, lodged in the self and selves that sign declarations.
Also: where is the love that is not for a person? Where is the love that is an ideal?
Flawed sapphire — your lady, the iron one, the rain washes her in storms,
and policemen protect her with assault weapons? No freedom without the sword,
I agree. No argument from me. I kiss the fantastic utopias in favour of topos.
I kiss your lady's sweet, beautiful, robed ass.
I worship the ground she walks on, *I love her*, because she would shelter me in the rain.

Crazy Shane, she coos, *Crazy Shane.*

Do *you* love her, have you touched her during the presidency of our disaffected
dreams? Citizens, the chained dream of softer chains and the ignorant dream of no pain
but the free dream of how to set the pain to the common good, in terms of the ones
they sleep with and by at night, the e pluribus unum coin of their realm, feeling flesh
that's carnal, generative, so deeply in love that it chafes at the chains

that it might set for itself, loving safety as much as it does. No safe place for *we*.
Your cities are set to burn in standard operating procedures written in glass,
thrown down from the Capitol mount or sunk in the same Hudson
that good Henry sampled in 1626 while Lenape elders took the sixty guilders
from the Guild of Ignorance and Alchemy, inaugurating the modern age of the brave
and free. Believe that if she cries for you, my iron lady erected near those ghosts,
it's not out of shame or embarrassment but because of the prophecy: the stones
are coming, the stones are coming. Freedom becomes the rain of those stones
on the glass palaces that brook no dissent of brothers, that shelter no others,
and the lady will do nothing but observe in the rain as palaces continue to fall.

I was like you, once

Eight years ago, the mirror in my vanity
caused my face to appear in mid-air,

                    disembodied.

                    Walt and I sing a song of ourselves on Broadway, "American Solipsism," democracy
                    and freedom admixed — the freedom to tyrannize ourselves in a definitional war.

In my bedroom eight years ago, I fantasized of the water
tower — to fall, free. It felt like love; I felt it as strong
as any other love. I know better now, but it passed as love
as I pass for normal. Now, I have no time to cry for myself,
only a hollowed-out space that sloshes with the internet's tears,
the worst of us groping for some diseased platform that blinks
a pixelated, brainscraping blue —

                                              They say *I support you*
                                     They mean *I screenshot your weakness*

Once, identity police said across the coffee table,

                                Yeah, like it's easy to say you're somewhere
                        on the neuroatypical scale somewhere as a straight white dude

and I said, *It's a spectrum, I agree. Where*
did I fall on the spectrum when I took a step
closer to the apartment ledge? Not very far.
What about when I was halfway down? I wish
there was a screenshot of my face from that moment.
Probably farther on the spectrum?
Where did I fall when I was a foot from the pavement?

Walt the bad, the bad, the bad — strung up by a theocracy

                    Grief walks through my soul's gate and says, *Walt's gone, they took him, he's deleted —*

The angel, running out the door again

Verse on the screen asked:

> *what difference could it make   to the angel*
> *built to monitor the Earth*

I didn't know —

in cell-agony, I asked the ten-year-old, who left the gray bungalow in New Brunswick and ran around the world only to jump back into my body the same night, "What difference does anything make?"

The ten-year-old angel said, "Despair is a mortal sin."

And all the words the helpfuls tried to share, the well-meaners — friends, people who truly care — flooded back as despair's noosey tongue:

You're his dad, that doesn't change;
the best you can do is be a good father.

I said, *And what difference does it make*
to the angel; my angel, me;

I agree but that

in us both are the words we heard our whole lives:

you're wrong, bad, bad, so bad — retarded — different —

Angel, you are a level for the world, suspended
at the selfsame angle of the boy's face in *La Coiffure* —
eye on the extant danger —

But how do we un-value the world as it was given to us?

What did you see during circumnavigation late one night that can cure me of curative thinking, of the diseased dreams of sameness —

Selfsame, the angel said to me, running out the door again

Love, love, love — can be made to be indistinguishable from abuse, in this world, and we no longer discern the beautiful things from pedagogy

The angel is at an invisible angle
The boy is at an invisible angle
but I have been corrected for so long —

so what is my love worth, now,
to him when it misses

Next to Edgar Allan Poe House and Museum, closed to the public for renovations

Doris Day:

> *Perfect ease we'll enjoy, without thinking to lend*
> *Ourselves to the world and its glee —*
> *Ever peaceful and blissful we'll be*

The boy:

> slumped in the chair, head tilted left,
> brown hair in his eyes, newly washed,
> sockless, trying to teach his sister
> about not being greedy —

Bronx ruminations:

> *I'm dying I'm dying I'm dying*
> *This is about me about me about me*

The boy:

> in the back seat teaching his sister
> about Ghost Town —
> *Aria, let's play Ghost Town!*

Kazuo = man of peace

Virginia Eliza:

> dead of pulmonary hemorrhage,
> *blinded with tears while writing*

Not love:

> not shed from love

Scripture in De Witt Clinton Park

And the angel of the Lord said unto him, Why askest thou thus after my name, seeing it is secret?

  —Judges 13:18

I once spoke of all the lamentations,
my son's medical history as litany.
Woe! a beautiful man interrupted, asked,
But what's his name?

The beautiful man was an angel;
his wings flapped in thunder,
rendering judgment.

I felt consumed from within
      — fire turned inward, no background to burn,
      my scorched core clearing material for creosote angels
      and mourning-space, where ashes are already ashes and dust is
      already dust —

My son is a green shoot, moved by goodgray wind;
I mustn't lose sight, yes.

Without asking, I knew the angel's name.
Though I knew he could overpower me,
that he was Jacob's angel — the selfsame —
I used what my mother taught me,
the word-cache that divines names.

I said, *You think your name is Love,*
as taught to you by God
but ask the earth, ask the earth,
ask all the people you judge and surveil.
They call you Mourning;
we call you Mourning.

Crossing Myself in Rutherford, NJ

After Paterson and the occluding press of people, a city as one long strip mall, we stopped the car in front of William Carlos Williams's house in Rutherford, still used by a doctor, oddly coloured, like an off-centre national dream, grayblue clapboard with red trim —

O national monument, I ask: what medicine are you made of?

— King Kong comes, plants huge Wal-Mart–sized stars and stripes on the lawn —

Yes, in the shadow of the flag, all things grow strange in that shade

In his autobiography, WCW wrote, "I do not intend to tell the particulars of the women I have been to bed with, or anything about them. Don't look for it. That has nothing to do with me." Meaning: he cheated, was bad, so bad, and others must tell us of his character defects, his errors —

I tried to be good, so good — I fell in love with a woman, I stayed with a woman, stayed in love, was true —

(And I was good)
(And it was good)

As aggrieved parent, I cross myself against medical error. Rather than label a disaster *miscommunication*, why not plainly say, *We didn't find in time the thing that ate most of a life*?

Would it help me to hear Truth at the cock crow?

(And I was good)
(And it was good)

Whole awakening republics of a rurality I once heard, lived in — crossing on awakening —

At night, I dream of children that hatch perfectly into WCW's smooth hands at Passaic General, he catches them as hell takes wing, like this:

> Once, *Why am I so sad?* was a luxurious, lolling question that languished for an answer;
> Then, *Why am I so sad?* made sense in terms of a childhood that, as an adult, seems to molt
>   into kindness for the self;
> Now, *Why am I so sad?* has good reasons, real ones —

Is it ableist to be angry in this context; to be sad, to rue my son's fate?

I ask you, house of good doctor Williams, as your haunting! I, the ghost of internalized ableism that hates what it was called when it was small and defenceless, when it was ten years old

Kate Zambreno in *O Fallen Angel*:

> *They always cross themselves and say, as if like a prayer*
>
> *It was nobody's fault*
> *It was nobody's fault*
> *. . . . .*
> *This allows them to be able to sleep at night*
> *to not be haunted*

There is fault, always fault — a role to play in all human affairs.

(And I was good)
(And it was good)

But whom does it help, thinking this way? National Monument, your Wal-Mart–sized flag makes forgiveness irrelevant. You billow a gangrenous freedom, blown by the wind that no longer makes the grass genuflect, a wind of despair

Your gate is in good repair, but the mortal sin that sponsors the nation is despair miscommunicated as freedom

Reformulation: *No ideas but in care, in relation*

I cross myself, I always do, some vestigial dream, and drive on, the oncoming Pennsylvania fields so beautiful, where we will be buried — some further field —

where the man sleeping in the furrows is a creosote angel sent by the internet to itemize all the injustice, but he's not dust but ash, not ash but dust, ahead of the wind, a grayblue lion, and he converts the injustice into joy, laughing at presumptive apocalypse, winking at the plurality,

it's Walt

The Hostage Tells a Love Story (Mental Health Check)

My children, I tell you of my father sitting on the deck in the rain, because there is no one else to tell what he told me, and no way to tell you *except* by this poor proxy.

The song I'm playing now is the same song, always the same, wrong for the moment —

Why tell? Because he's how anyone can be. You turn up the music, or sit in the rain with an indoor stereo dragged outside, and no help that you'll let near because — who else could understand?

I tell because the practice of monsters is to reconvene.

Look now: Zee with silver-shock hair and arched lip reclines on the circular sectional; Kaz of the joyous laugh jumps on the battered couch; rounded Aria hugs her sister's leg.

Listen!

You, too, will find yourself listening in the rain soon, with beautiful music.

My father's in the rain and there's no helping him. He sat while his concert-sized Technics blared so the whole street heard his loneliness sounding theirs.

Like you, I wanted to sleep in my bed, to make it through a night without the police following up on a complaint from the neighbours, who knew better than to come near. And if that is fear, then it is a fear I felt, like tonguing metal on a New Brunswick winter night.

He screamed for me to come, worse if I didn't;
                                      I tried to ignore the sound, but it sounded me
under the blankets, and I knew it would hurt
                                      more, in the end, if I didn't walk outside
in the gentle rain where he sat alone and still,
                                      with kingly knowledge on a plastic
throne, pointing at *Havoc* in the distance.
                                      Then, children, he was what I was always,
what *we* were, what I'd become as his summoned,
                                      screamed extension: the metal tool, the hard
implement, the feeling that prepares the field.
                                      But the moment did not last. He could see
I was too small to understand and sent me back.

Young ones, if your faces are the lifeline of my free future, then his face from that night
is the ruin of a memory I never wanted but couldn't   flee.

Like him, I lack the vocabulary to explain why lives seek gentleness in the steady rain.
Try to explain the need and you'll find yourself out in the rain.

For example: *Hey, be with me*, I'd think at my lovers, but they were always with themselves
or with their own monsters. Was I ever with them?

On the deck, in the noise, my father was content, in some future he never knew. Having done wrong
in his past, he wove song into a cocoon of sound, a shelter of sorts.

I have no words now except one, my children, the word of the metal feeling:

>   *Run.*

That's my father's sound, his voice and voices speaking from the deck in the rain, telling me
that love stories don't make sense on purpose so that no one will believe, including the lovers;
that the teller wouldn't believe before his telling; that love stories hinge on sudden, doomed
transformation, unable to change back after the story can't be fixed, with poor choices leading
to bitter ends,

but it's still love. This is the feeling, the song's metal whine and thrum.

All my father's missed chances to tell the world *Thank you* and *Sorry* and *I miss you* and *I will
always help you, I care for you, I love you, I love you so* —

stories he told by himself in the rain as the police came with a citation; stories monsters
whispered in his ear about loveliness and narcotics, all of us powerless

to stop the song.

Acknowledgements

This poetic archive of wisdom extended from a disabled man to his children owes thanks to Walt Whitman, Zee, Kaz, Aria, dis/ability, and every line I have ever read. Always: compassion to the suffering person! Let *that* be your process and praxis in this world, the same one in which we have so little time together. There is no thanking Jim Johnstone. Let me thank Gary Barwin who, after witnessing my grief, sent me a photo of this bit of Geoffrey Hill from *The Triumph of Love*:

> So — Croker, MacSikker, O'Shem — I ask you:
> what are poems for? They are to console us
> with their own gift, which is like perfect pitch.
> Let us commit that to our dust. What
> ought a poem to be? Answer, *a sad*
> *and angry consolation*. What is
> the poem? What figures? Say,
> *a sad and angry consolation*. That's
> beautiful. Once more? *A sad and angry*
> *consolation*.

I have said so.

As selected by Margaret Atwood and Jordan Abel, "Epistemology" won the Walrus Poetry Prize in 2017.

The *Walrus* published "Deep Religious Faith" in 2020.

The *Fiddlehead* published "Shame-Trick," "Obligation-Trick," "Fear-Trick," and "Freedom-Trick" in its 2018 Summer Poetry Issue and (with slight variations in the titles) "My heart breaks in the NYPL, but it was already broken, truly — I just stumbled on the pieces," "Scripture in De Witt Clinton Park," and "e pluribus unum per cent" in the 2020 Summer Poetry Issue. That the fern remains is one of the constancies I continue to cherish.

The FOLD 2020 festival programme reprinted "Obligation-Trick."

Canadian Literature published "Death-Trick" in 2019.

Poetry published "In the famous American art gallery" and "Fatherhood-Trick" in 2020.

JAMA published "One's Self I Sing, Too" in 2020.

The Blasted Tree published "The Hostage Tells a Love Story" as a pamphlet in 2020.

Filling Station published "Never-Trick" and "No-Trick" in 2020.

Event published "Faithless in Hospitals" in 2021.

The *Dalhousie Review* published "Driving across Pennsylvania, I Had a Great Notion" (as "Driving across Pennsylvania and Sheryl Crow Comes on the Radio") and "To All My Followers, I Propose the Photosynthesis-Dopamine Hypothesis" in 2020.

"At the Met to Die Again" was shortlisted for the Montreal International Poetry Prize and published as "At the Met to Get Wrecked" by Véhicule Press in the *2020 Montreal Poetry Prize Anthology*.

Knife | Fork | Book published "Whitman on Twitter," "My Heart Broke in the New York Public Library," and "I was like you, once" in the chapbook *Walt* (2021).

"The Weeping Tense" was published in 2021 in *Vallum* and *Anomaly* (US).

The author acknowledges the generous support of the Ontario Arts Council.

ONTARIO ARTS COUNCIL
CONSEIL DES ARTS DE L'ONTARIO
an Ontario government agency
un organisme du gouvernement de l'Ontario

Shane Neilson is a poet from New Brunswick. His father was born in Sheffield, New Brunswick; his mother, in what used to be known as Newcastle. Shane writes a great deal on poetry and medicine.

Photo by Hannah Marie